Top 10 Business Lessons Through
An Inspiring Life Of
A Visionary Entrepreneur

ELON MUSK

The Man With A Quest To
Change The World's Future

_EntrepreneurshipFacts.com

All information contained within this book has been researched from reputable sources. If any information is found to be false, please contact the publisher, who will be happy to make corrections for future editions.

Follow EntrepreneurshipFacts on social media to stay updated with our free book promotions and increase your knowledge about business and successful people on a daily basis:

Instagram   Facebook   Twitter

Also check out our website for the latest facts and articles about business and entrepreneurship:

www.EntrepreneurshipFacts.com

Table Of Contents

Introduction 5

Short Biography 7

Lesson #1– On Seizing Opportunity 13

Lesson # 2 – On Purpose 24

Lesson # 3 – On Failure 31

Lesson # 4 – On Criticism 38

Lesson # 5 – On Hiring 47

Lesson # 6 – On Perseverance 55

Lesson # 7 – On Hard Work 62

Lesson # 8 – On having Fun 69

Lesson # 9 – On Changing the World 77

Lesson # 10 – On the Future 82

Conclusion 92

Introduction

Elon Musk is a man unlike any other. His world-changing ideas are altering the course of human industry, making him famous as an investor, inventor, entrepreneur and engineer. Although he has changed the world in many ways, he is probably best known for his position at the head of Tesla Motors, SolarCity, and SpaceX. Musk is a visionary, who has revolutionized several industries in only a few years.

Many believe that he is an engineer above all other engineers, with a mind more brilliant than any other industrial mind in this century. You may never have heard of Musk, but even if not, he has likely developed inventions and innovations that have affected your life, or the lives of those you know.

This book examines some of Elon Musk's famous quotes and analyzes the meaning and significance of each quote. Along with each quote is the real life story of how Elon Musk himself implements those same principles effectively in his life and business.

Short Biography

Elon Musk entered the world in 1971 in the country of South Africa. He was the first of three children born to his father, an engineer, and his mother, a model. His siblings were socially "in", part of the group, but Elon Musk felt more like an outsider. He would spend his time reading comics and books, avoiding the kids who bullied him for being smart.

Musk developed a fascination with programming, and took a few classes. The classes proved a bit of a disappointment because Musk was way more advanced than his teacher. By the time he was 12, Musk had taught himself to program computers, trying out his ideas on a video game he created and named Blastar. He went on to sell this new invention for 500 dollars.

When Musk was 17, he moved to Canada. Later he relocated again, ending up at the University of Pennsylvania in the US. After his graduation from the University of Pennsylvania, Musk went on to California, where he enrolled in classes in physics at Stanford University. His graduate studies focused on his main interest: exploring space. However after only two days had passed, before he barely got started, Musk decided to drop his classes and leave the university to see if he could make money from the current internet boom.

It didn't take long for Musk to start his own company. Zip2, Musk's first company proved profitable, offering newspapers online, complete with business directories and maps. In 1999, he sold Zip2 to Compaq for 22 million dollars. That same year, he started X.com (which later changed its name to PayPal), a company that allowed people to make payments online. He got 180 million out of the deal when eBay bought the company in exchange for 1.5 billion dollars' worth of stock.

Moving on from the internet world, Musk founded a new company, Space Exploration Technologies (more commonly known as SpaceX) in 2002. This new company completely changed the way people thought about vehicle creation. More specifically, SpaceX focused on developing rocket technology. It was Musk's hope to reduce costs for space flights to such a degree that the ordinary individual could afford to make a trip into space, spreading out human life and viability to regions beyond Planet

Earth. Musk's initial attempts to get funding for his new venture failed, so he invested all the savings he had into building SpaceX. Despite people's original misgivings about Musk's project, he proved so successful that currently NASA has made a 1.6 billion dollar contract with SpaceX. NASA's hope is that by investing their money into SpaceX, this company will be able to transport people to and from the International Space Station.

Not long after he founded SpaceX, Musk went on to fund Tesla Motors, a company committed to develop cars run by electricity. The Tesla Roadster appeared as the company's first car. This car changed the concept the general population held regarding electric cars. While people used to think of electric cars as something that could not be done and made practical, now people began to see it as a viable possibility. As of 2016, Tesla has produced several different models of electric cars, and is hoping to be able to offer electric cars to the public at prices that average people can afford.

Musk's ingenuity is shown in many ways. The Hyperloop, introduced by Musk in 2013, is designed to be able to transport people between Los Angeles and San Francisco in only 30 minutes, using pressurized tubes. The Tesla Powerwall, created by Musk's company is a simple battery, created to allow homes to be powered off the main electricity grid. Besides coming up with his own inventions, Musk also is one of the main drivers behind SolarCity, which was founded by his cousins. In 2016, Tesla made a bid to buy SolarCity. The deal would transform Tesla from a maker of cars and batteries into a clean energy powerhouse - making not only cars and batteries, but entire energy generation systems.

Moreover, In 2013, Fortune named Musk "Business Person of the Year" for his work with Tesla,

SolarCity, and SpaceX, and Esquire Magazine has included him in their list of the "75 Most Influential People of the 21st Century".

Lesson #1– On Seizing Opportunity

"The first step is to establish that something is possible; then probability will occur."

Quote context:

Interview with Tom Junod for Esquire Magazine, issue December 2012

Meaning of the quote:

Never leave anything to chance. There are always things you can do to increase the likelihood of positive serendipity. Some people dream of success, claiming that they are capable of great things, but ultimately settle down with far less. They then justify it with excuses, for example that there are not enough opportunities out there or that their talents are somehow restricted.

Opportunities never come rolling out of nowhere, just like luck does not happen by chance. Blaming the circumstances of one's own life, upbringing or background is futile. As Bruce Lee once said, "To hell with circumstances, I create opportunities." Chance or luck has to be created. Once it is created, then the possibilities will come. Therefore, the first thing one must do to create opportunities is to believe that it is possible. In particular, if the Wright brothers did not believe that humans could fly, then they would not have invented the world's first airplane.

Lessons from Elon Musk:

It's easy to assume that Musk had it made for him, and that he automatically was born to be successful. After all, he started successful internet businesses, Zip2 and the popular PayPal, early in his career. How could any normal man accomplish such a feat? But despite all such illusions and impressions, Musk began life with a large handicap that could have destroyed the dreams of most people with less determination and initiative.

What were some of Musk's early handicaps? As a child, the general South African culture was not easy on him. He lived with his father, a man known to be harsh to his children. Not only that, bullies tormented Musk at school. These children tortured Musk and made him hate the school environment. Once, they beat him up so badly that he had to go to the hospital and was not able to go back to school for a whole week.

"They got my best fucking friend to lure me out of hiding so they could beat me up. And that fucking hurt. For some reason they decided that I was it, and they were going to go after me nonstop. That's what made growing up difficult. For a number of years there was no respite. You get chased around by gangs at school who tried to beat the shit out of me, and then I'd come home, and it would just be awful there as well."

As Musk grew up and personal computers made their advent, he began spending hours playing on these new devices, discover new and innovative ways to use computers, way above and beyond the ability that any of his fellow students possessed. At 16, Elon Musk and Kimbal, his brother, tried out an idea and opened a video arcade at a spot near where they attended high school. Their venture was shut down by the city even though they had a lease on the property. This corruption in the city management, a problem that plagued the whole country, was disturbing to both of the Musk brothers.

Musk was so frustrated; he decided to leave the country. South Africa didn't line up with his ideologies, and didn't offer his creative mind the opportunities it needed to grow and develop to its full potential. The country was split by Apartheid, and if he stayed in South Africa, Musk knew the fate that would befall him: he would be required to serve in the military in this country that he did not even feel loyal to. As Musk later stated:

"Suppressing black people didn't seem like a good way to spend my time."

Once Musk graduated from high school, he made up his mind: he would travel to the USA and make a new home there. Musk was prepared for such a move. He had researched and done the homework, realizing that starting as an immigrant from South Africa, it would be difficult to obtain US citizenship. But, seeing the obstacle, he also found a way to get around it. Since his mother had been born in Canada, he could easily obtain a Canadian citizenship. Before he turned 18, Musk left South Africa and never returned. He made his new home in Canada, hoping that this step would help him gain access into the US.

Despite all the planning that Musk had done, there were a few things he had not anticipated. His original plan was to live with his great uncle in Montreal. Since it was back in 1988, Musk used a payphone to call his uncle after he arrived in Canada, but no answer. What could he do? He then called his mom, Maye, back in South Africa to see if she had any updated information on his uncle's whereabouts. She did, but it was not good news. She had received a letter while Musk was on his way to the US. Apparently his uncle had moved to Minnesota. As a result, Musk would not be able to live with him after all.

Musk then has to come up with a plan B. He remembered that his mother had other relatives in different parts of Canada, he began contacting them. For a sum of 100 dollars, he was able to buy a special ticket that allowed him to ride buses across the country, getting on and off whenever he wanted. Almost 2000 miles later, he arrived in a town called Swift Current. A second cousin of his lived there, so he called him up with no advanced warning, and managed to catch a ride to his house.

Musk's next task was to work and earn money, so he got random jobs around the country, tending vegetables, shoveling grain out of bins, cutting logs with a chain saw, and more. The hardest of the jobs, in Musk's opinion, was cleaning a lumber mill's boiler.

Although work had taken Musk to Vancouver, British Columbia, in 1989, he enrolled in Queen's University, located in Kingston, Ontario. Not long afterwards, Musk's brother also escaped to Canada, and the two would spend the evenings together, reading the newspaper. Musk and his brother not only spent time together reading, but also did more adventuresome and mischievous things, like cold-calling individuals they wished they could meet, for example, Peter Nicholson, a top executive in the

Bank of Nova Scotia. They actually landed a meeting with Nicholson, and began a relationship. Over the years, Nicholson became one of Musk's trusted advisors. Nicholson later told about how the friendship began: "I was not in the habit of getting out-of-the-blue requests. I was perfectly prepared to have lunch with a couple of kids that had that kind of gumption."

Musk paid his own way through university, using creative ideas to get the money he needed. He sold PC computer parts, as well as whole computers while he was in the dorm, as a means of getting a little extra in his pockets. He would also troubleshoot computer problems for fellow students, including problems with viruses or booting the computer. Not only this, he could create machines for the other students. The machines that Musk created for them would do what they needed done; and better yet, Musk would sell the machines he invented to his fellow students for less than they could get something similar at the store.

After two years at Queen's University, Musk transferred his studies to a US university, the University of Pennsylvania, where he had a scholarship. Musk believed that this Ivy League school might open some new doors, and so he decided to pursue two degrees, one in economics at the Wharton School, and subsequently a bachelor's degree in physics.

Musk continued to employ creative ways to fund his college venture, renting an off campus frat house with a friend that was large enough to turn into a night club on the weekends. By charging their fellow students five dollars every time they came, they were able to cover their entire month's rent in one single night of activity.

Once Musk graduated, he and Kimbal, his brother, decided to make the most of the dotcom era, and began to thrive, allowing Musk to become the famous person he is today. His astounding ideas are not merely fantasy, but are grounded in his vision and knowledge. Although his dream of going to Mars may seem unlikely, it has allowed him to take huge strides close to home, and even in outer space. It's Musk's will that explains who he is and how he's gotten this far. His first wife Justine (the mother of his five kids) goes so far as to state, ***"Elon is not afraid of breaking things — he will break himself if he has to."***

Lesson # 2 – On Purpose

"Going from PayPal, I thought: 'Well, what are some of the other problems that are likely to most affect the future of humanity?' Not from the perspective, 'What's the best way to make money?"

Quote context:

Commencement speech at The California Institute of Technology (Caltech)
2012 Commencement, June 15, 2012

Meaning of the quote:

Why you're doing something is important. So often in this world where we live, people are focused on results, or more specifically, focused on the money that's in any given job. After all, you do need money to live, so this has continued to be important to many people. But it's never enough to truly satisfy. Money can never fill your deepest cravings. We were made for something better, for a purpose that is higher than simply money. When we pursue something that is really worth living for, it makes us eager to get up in the mornings, and motivates us to worker hard and better each day that passes.

No one can legitimately say money is insignificant, but it is equally clear that having a purpose higher than just money is crucial to feeling fulfilled, and even contributes to how much happiness you can find in the work environment. Interestingly enough, several companies that fulfill purpose also become the most profitable. For example, Google organizes the information of the world that is scattered across the internet, making it useful and accessible to most people. Steve Job is another great example. In 1980, he declared that his mission statement for his company, Apple, was: "To make a contribution to the world by making tools for the mind that advance humankind."

Lessons from Elon Musk:

When people would ask him what he wanted to do when he grew up, as a child, Musk didn't really know what to answer. His passions developed over time, as he read. One quote that motivated him was a statement from Arthur C. Clark, "A sufficiently advanced technology is indistinguishable from magic."

In the 1980s, when most people didn't know the first thing about turning on a computer, Musk began to learn programming as a young child. He wanted to take classes at first, but he was so far ahead of his teachers that he resorted to teaching himself. By the time he was 12, he created Blastar, his own video game. Although he *was able to sell it for 500 dollars, money was never his primary goal. He loved inventing things, and money often followed.*

Similarly, when the Internet became so popular in the 90s, Musk didn't want to let the opportunity pass him. He determined to develop something that would be useful for those using the Internet. Together with his brother, Musk developed Zip2, a system similar to the old yellow pages—offering software to newspaper companies that allowed them to see who lived where.

When this initial Internet venture proved successful, Musk sold it to another company, Compaq Computer, in 1999. It went for $307 million, and of that Musk received 15 million, and his brother 22 million (in US dollars). Having become a multi-millionaire through the sale, Musk aimed higher. He wanted to do more than help newspaper companies. He wanted to invent something that could change the world.

Musk invested the money he had made off of Zip2 into the next big project he undertook, X.com. His plans for this company were to make it a hub of financial services where various types of service types could be integrated smoothly together. As he pursued these plans, he quickly realized that people were more interested in one particular feature, making payments online. Seeing this, he turned his focus in this direction, allowing X.com to evolve into what we now know as PayPal, a leader among the online payment systems of the world.

PayPal changed people's ways of paying for things, as well as how they transferred money from person to person in fundamental ways. To get a better view of how radically it changed things, at the time of its invention, it was still normal for individuals to mail checks in the mail to pay for what they owed. This was not only slow, but is now seen as an archaic process, and it could take several weeks to finish just one transaction.

When eBay acquired the company in 2002, Musk got 307 million out of the 1.5 billion dollar deal. Musk had set out to change the financial industry, and had made himself extremely rich in the process. Musk had more than he could ever need to live in luxury once he retired, but he had no plans to stop exploring new things. He still had dreams of changing the way humanity was going. He began to ponder:

"The biggest terrestrial problem is sustainable energy. Production and consumption of energy in a sustainable

manner. If we don't solve that in this century, we're in deep trouble. And the other thing I thought might affect humanity is the idea of making life multi-planetary."

He took these two dreams, and out of the first of them, Tesla (and SolarCity) was born, while the second gave birth to SpaceX. Musk dreams big, not starting with ideas he came up with randomly some day, or even by analyzing the market to see where there was a gap that would allow him to exploit the system. Rather, he dreams of advancing the human race, taking them places they've never been before, and bettering the world we call our home.

Lesson # 3 – On Failure

"Failure is an option here. If things are not failing, you are not innovating enough."

Quote context:

Interview with Jennifer Reingold, a Fast Company senior writer for an article about SpaceX featured in the Fast Company magazine, issue February 2005.

Meaning of the quote:

How many of us learned to walk the very first time we ever tried? The answer of course, is none of us. We all acknowledge that a child becomes successful at walking by taking risks and learning from their failed attempts. So we still enthusiastically encourage the attempts regardless of how many times the child falls; if the child is not falling at all, it means they are not trying. This ultimately means they'll never succeed at walking.

The same process must be continued for the rest of our lives. Rather than come to view failure as a social stigma, as something to be avoided at all costs, as a loss greater than the learning benefits, it should be viewed as just another stepping stone towards success. Fear of failure only leads to inaction. As Albert Einstein once said, *"A person who never made a mistake never tried anything new."* If you are innovating, failing is inevitable.

Lessons from Elon Musk:

Remarkable as it might seem, one man with a few outstanding ideas can change the space industry, disrupting the usual flow of one of the most difficult existing industries in the world. If Elon Musk had been a graduate in the field of space science, maybe you could have explained this phenomenon, but Musk began SpaceX with almost no experience whatsoever. His background was in business and software engineering, totally different than developing rocket science.

With the goal of colonizing Mars and developing technologies that could drastically cut space transportation expenses, he founded the SpaceX business in 2002. In his early ventures with this program, Musk approached the Russian space program several times, hoping to buy one of their refurbished rockets off of them to have something to start his company and put wings to his space dreams. Much to his disappointment, the Russian space program turned down his request all three times.

Not only were the Russians skeptical, but potential investors were as well. They refused to contribute to the idea, thinking it was just something he had dreamed up that would come to nothing. Private travel to space seemed so far beyond what anyone could imagine, so Musk had to fund much of his work himself. He created a backup plan, so in case his extravagant space plans failed, the company itself would not lose too much.

> *"If we don't get the first SpaceX rocket launch to succeed by the time we've spent 100 million dollars, we will stop the company. That will be enough for three attempted launches."*

The first launch was a failure, using a staggering 30 million in the process. The second launch likewise failed after Musk and the company had spent 60 million dollars. There was only one more time before Musk would have to surrender to failure. But thankfully, that third try succeeded! Seeing that

SpaceX had potential, NASA made a contract with them for 1.6 billion dollars, employing them to shuttle supplies to the International Space station.

Happy with his success, Elon Musk didn't stop creating. He determined to develop a reusable launch method so that the rockets could successfully come back to earth and be reused, thus greatly reducing the cost of going to space. While this concept had been a dream that people in the space industry had long played with, no one really thought it could ever work—or at least no one had been able to come up with any strategy that made the dream of reusable rocket technology feasible.

Musk's original attempts did not succeed any better than anyone else's. In 2015, SpaceX made three failed attempts to re-land their Falcon 9 models after they were launched. The third time, not only did the landing after launch not succeed, but the rocket exploded after its failed landing attempt.

Millions of dollars were lost in the process. Despite the failures and loss of finances, SpaceX was learning a lot, and each time brought them closer to their goal and taught them priceless information about what to change for the next attempt.

Finally, in December of 2015, SpaceX made its first successful rocket landing after a launch. The rocket came in and landed upright for the very first time in human history. In April of 2016, only four months later, SpaceX set another record in human history, vertically landing a rocket on a platform floating out in the ocean. When Musk was asked if he would consider giving up he replied:

"No, I don't ever give up. I'd have to be dead or completely incapacitated."

Lesson # 4 – On Criticism

"It's very important to actively seek out and listen very carefully to negative feedback. This is something people tend to avoid because it's painful, but I think this is a very common mistake."

Quote context:

Interview with Kevin Rose for the Foundation Show on the website foundation.kr, released September 7, 2012.

Meaning of the quote:

We should understand that all ideas can be improved no matter how good they already are. An essential part of succeeding at ideas and projects lies in one's own ability to develop the emotional wherewithal to accept criticism.

Criticism is like exercise. It sucks in the beginning. But failure it is the best teacher of all. While compliments create contentment, criticism creates improvement. So whenever you receive criticism, evaluate whether the "negative" criticism has value to you, learn from it, and act upon it.

Lessons from Elon Musk:

While Tesla Motors was not founded directly by Musk, but rather by Martin Eberhard and Marc Tarpenning (in 2003), Musk entered the company early-on in its development, joining the Board of Directors in 2004. From the time Musk began investing in the company and joined the leadership, he had a goal, a vision for Tesla to be more than an ordinary automobile company. He hoped that in time, the company could mass-produce electronic cars that even average people could afford.

Before Musk came onto the scene, electric cars were considered to be eccentric and unusual—no one really took the thought seriously. Some even went so far as to criticize Musk for investing in such an endeavor which they were certain would fail. To prove to their critics that the electric car was viable, Tesla Motors built something that went above and beyond the traditional gas-propelled car in every way.

The company's first car, the Tesla Roadster, designed personally by Musk, received the Global Green 2006 Product Design Award. The hard work of overseeing each component of styling, headlights, the power electronics, and more had paid off! But there were problems too; things that would have to be corrected before the car could be efficient to be sold on a large scale.

By the end of the launch night, after giving test rides to potential customers, the car already had very negative reviews, and some cars were dismantled. Musk acknowledged these accusations, and went on to improve the model.

Investors and entrepreneurs saw potential, and began to invest in Tesla. In 2007, Sergei Brin and Larry Page, co-founders of Google contributed significantly to the company. Irony, when Musk tried to give these two donors a ride in the Roadster model, the car wouldn't go over 10 miles per hour.

Jeremy Clarkson, from Top Gear reviewed two Roadsters in 2008, and declared that they were a "barely-running science experiment that couldn't survive a full day at the Top Gear track". Sadly, that year also coincided with the world's great financial crisis, forcing the company to fire one tenth of their workforce. To their chagrin, some of their best personnel who had helped to start the company also were eliminated by necessity. In connection with this disaster, Musk became the company's new CEO. By investing 17 million of his own money into the company, he felt confident that he could develop an improved version of electric car that would meet the demands of the population.

The government saw some potential in the company, and in 2009, the US Government extended a large loan to Tesla to support the engineering of the Model S sedan. Tesla was so successful, that by 2013, they were able to repay the loan. Meanwhile, Nissan and Ford, who had received the same loan from the government still hadn't repaid theirs. In early 2009, Tesla revealed their all-electric sedan, the Model S. By 2010, Tesla began selling their vehicles to the public, making them the first American car producers since Ford to take this step.

While the Tesla's Model S proved to be much cheaper and better than their earlier cars, it still proved out of the price range of many, at 52,400 dollars. Bub Lutz, a former executive at General Motors claimed that this was a car only for luxury. In July of 2012 he stated that the Model S was "a nice car for a social elite". Musk took everything in measure. He stated:

"When I spoke with someone about the Tesla Model S, I didn't really want to know what's right about the car. I want to know what's wrong about the car"

Tesla kept pressing ahead, and in 2015 released an all-electric crossover SUV, the Tesla X. The vehicle's overall impression proved only slightly better than that of its predecessors, and was still very expensive. There were also a few safety issues, which resulted in more than 2000 vehicles being recalled by Tesla Motors, who admitted that the release had come prematurely.

Despite different frustrating car releases, Tesla pressed ahead, releasing the Tesla Model 3 in 2016. This car proved to be a huge success, an endgame car for Tesla; a car that made electric cars have a fighting chance in the mainstream car market. Better yet, the price was reasonable: 35,000 dollars. After the introduction of the Model 3, Tesla received 276,000 preorders, with a deposit of $1000 for each, in just 72 hours. For the first time, electric cars began to sell en masse.

One benefit of this new car was its noiseless performance—with no roar of a gas burning engine and no vibrations, the car speeds smoothly, silently over the roads. Using electricity makes it friendly to the environment, and its torque and acceleration are instantaneous, giving it an edge on competitors. The car's unique bearing distribution and low center of gravity allow ease in handling, and it has a 5-star safety rating; only one percent of cars can claim similar safety levels.

With Elon's willingness to accept criticism and to work diligently to fix the errors he had made in previous car models, he attained his dream at last—a practical mass-market electric car, available at prices the general public can afford.

"I think it's very important to have a feedback loop, where you're constantly thinking about what you've done and how you could be doing it better. I think that's the single best piece of advice: constantly think about how you could be doing things better and questioning yourself."

Lesson # 5 – On Hiring

"The most important thing is to attract great people. Either join a group that's amazing that you really respect, or if you're building a company, you've gotta gather great people."

Quote context:

Commencement speech at The University of Southern California (USC) 2014 Commencement

Meaning of the quote:

Employees are the heart and soul of a business; they are the mechanism that makes a business run; they are the breath of life that enables a business to be something more than an idea. A business cannot run unless someone is doing the work. Any business owner hopes to have talented employees.

The most successful business owners in the world will tell you there is nothing more important than hiring right employees, and firing bad employees quickly. Because hiring the right people can make or break your company, sometimes you have to look past their talent and rely on your intuition. Talent alone is not enough to determine a great employee. Work ethic and personality can outweigh talent, as skills can be trained but not personality.

Lessons from Elon Musk:

With his excellent track record in so many careers, Musk obviously has skills in leading organizations and choosing which employees to hire. His skill in evaluating people's abilities and capabilities in interviews is superb. He knows how to choose people who will back up the company's reputation and culture, and how to find the right individual for each specific role, some of the most important things to look for when hiring.

Naturally, talented and skilled people will be attracted to someone like Musk, because qualified people tend to seek out other high-quality people to work with. However this is not the only thing that is important to Elon Musk. What other types of characteristics is he looking for in someone he hires? What kind of qualities must a person have for Musk to choose him or her to help translate his dreams into real life, to be employed at one of his companies that has such large aspirations that they are literally out of this planet?

There are several factors Musk takes into consideration. One of the most important is commitment—someone who is just as dedicated to the mission as Musk himself is, someone willing to sacrifice years of time with family, and good sleep in order to fulfil the dream.

If there is one word that describes the companies that Musk leads, it is the word "intense". Musk himself stated regarding his mars mission with SpaceX:

> *"SpaceX is like Special Forces... we do the missions that others think are impossible. We have goals that are absurdly ambitious by any reasonable standard, but we're going to make them happen. We have the potential here at SpaceX to have an incredible effect on the future of humanity and life itself."*

A similar statement could be made about Tesla. The jobs these companies offer are not the typical nine to five job that many are seeking. Musk said of those who work at Tesla:

> *"You will be expected to challenge and to be challenged, to create, and to innovate. These jobs are not for everyone, you must have a genuine passion for producing the best vehicles in the world. Without passion, you will find what we're trying to do too difficult."*

Obviously, Elon Musk is seeking people who are as committed to electric cars and space travel as he is. That is way more important to him than a good resume or even a technical background. He knows from experience that when you have a mind to do something, you can learn as you go. That is what he's looking for in others too: people committed to working long shifts, with little outside structure and not that much training. He believes employees should be able to figure it out on their own.

In return for what he asks of people, he compensates them well financial. His dreams are ambitious. With all these factors at play, an overwhelming number of individuals turn in resumes, seeking employment at Musk's companies. Because of this, the interviewing process at both SpaceX and Tesla are intense. One applicant, for example, stated that part of his screening included a coding test that lasted for six hours.

Applicants go through lengthy interviews with many people asking them very specific questions about their past experiences in order to assess the level of knowledge the applicants possess, and what their intellectual abilities are.

This is only the beginning. If applicants pass these initial interviews, they have to pass one final hurdle: talking to the famous Elon Musk himself. Musk personally interviews each person they intend to hire to SpaceX, even though there are over 500 employed there.

He asks potential employees to explain their career history, their decision making process when important things are at stake, and how they've handled tough problems in the past. If they have solved problems, he asks more questions to find out the details, because Musk claims that those who have figured out problems personally will remember in great detail what was wrong and how they corrected the situation. This allows Musk to sift out any who may be claiming problem-solving skills that they do not really have. Musk also probes into the candidate's accomplishments.

Lesson # 6 – On Perseverance

"If something is important enough, even if the odds are against you, you should still do it."

Quote context:

With Sheila Hibbard, for themarketingbit.com (Marketing – 5 Lessons from Big Idea Guy, Elon Musk) published October 15, 2012

Meaning of the quote:

For serious entrepreneurs, their business is their life's blood. It feeds them and they feed it. Drive and determination are what will keep them and their business going. No successful business achieved real success without facing setbacks. In fact, that's what all of us will face in our lives: obstacle after obstacle.

The only difference between winners and losers is not whether one has failed or succeeded, but how they reacted in the face of failure; how the winners got back up and kept going because of the importance of what they were doing. Perseverance is what ultimately allowed the winners to reach the finish line.

Lessons from Elon Musk:

If you're a small business owner, the companies that Musk established, SpaceX and Tesla, likely seem completely beyond your reach. That's beside the point. The reality is, Elon Musk started out very small, with basically nothing. Not only that, he was a foreigner in a foreign country, without much money or many contacts. Through his dedication, planning, and especially through his perseverance, Musk proved himself successful over and over in areas of industry where it seems impossible to succeed.

Let's look at Musk's story of developing SpaceX from another point of view.

Musk's coworkers say that when the man begins a project, he puts a lot of thought into it, making a clearly stated goal, and examining why that goal is valid and good. Once he has his goal in place, he sets out to learn everything he can on the topic under discussion, drawing information from multiple sources.

His sources include both books, articles, and others with experience in that domain. His colleagues in the rocket science field lend him books, he confers with others about potential rocket designs over his lunch break, and he even hires people with expertise to give him advice. Those who interact with him claim that he absorbs knowledge from the people surrounding him, not only because he's intelligent, but also because he's determined, seeking tenaciously to learn whatever he can.

On quora.com, Jim Cantrell, who helped Musk found SpaceX, answered the question: "How did Elon Musk manage to learn enough about rockets to run SpaceX?" Cantrell answered:

> *"I am going to suggest that he is successful not because his visions are grand, not because he is extraordinarily smart and not because he works incredibly hard. All of those things are true. The one major important distinction that sets him apart is his inability to consider failure. It simply is not even in his thought process. He cannot conceive of failure and that is truly remarkable.*

"It doesn't matter if it's going up against the banking system (PayPal), going up against the entire aerospace industry (SpaceX) or going up against the US auto industry (Tesla). He can't imagine NOT succeeding and that is a very critical trait that leads him ultimately to success.

"He and I had very similar upbringings, very similar interests and very similar early histories. He was a bit of a loner and so was I. He decided to start a software company at age 13. I decided to design and build my own stereo amplifier system at age 13. Both of us succeeded at it. We both had engineers for fathers and were extremely driven kids.

"What separated us, I believe, was his lack of even being able to conceive failure. I know this because this is where we parted ways at SpaceX. We got to a point where I could not *see it succeeding and walked away. He didn't and succeeded. I have 25 years' experience building space hardware and he had none at the time. So much for experience."*

Although Musk refused to believe in the possibility of failure, both his major companies, Tesla Motors and SpaceX almost failed at one point or another. The Roadster, the first electric car Tesla produced, had many problems, causing the company to struggle substantially when the financial crash in 2008 occurred. SpaceX also had three failed launches before they made a successful launch on the fourth try. Besides all this, in Musk's personal life, he was facing a divorce. These events all happened so close together that he nearly had a mental breakdown.

But Musk kept going. Through sheer determination and the choice to persevere at all costs, he met his goals, succeeding in areas where others failed. His life's story is perfectly aligned with a famous quote from Steve Jobs, the founder of Apple: "I'm convinced that about half of what separates the successful entrepreneurs from the non-successful ones is pure perseverance."

Lesson # 7 – On Hard Work

"Work like hell. I mean you just have to put in 80 to 100 hour weeks every week. [This] improves the odds of success. If other people are putting in 40 hour work weeks and you're putting in 100 hour work weeks, then even if you're doing the same thing you know that… you will achieve in 4 months what it takes them a year to achieve."

Quote context:

Interview with Vator News in 2013

Meaning of the quote:

A dream doesn't become reality through magic; it takes sweat, determination and hard work. Success is no accident. It is hard work, perseverance, sacrifice and most of all you have to be passionate about what you are doing.

If you think about it, the only thing in life you really have full control over is your own effort. You might feel demotivated or uninspired at times, as these are things which are sometimes difficult to control. But in business, nothing will happen unless you make it happen. "Work like there is someone working 24 hours a day to take it away from you" is a famous quote from billionaire Mark Cuban. In fact, it is true that there is always someone out there who is working hard every day to compete with you; and if you do not work hard, you will soon go out of business.

Lessons from Elon Musk:

Most people know that hard work is an important element of success, but how can Musk continue his pace of working between 85 and 100 hours each week? Not only does he work at that rate now, he has for more than a decade, managing both Tesla and SpaceX, and overseeing other large projects such as Hyperloop and SolarCity. How has Elon Musk developed the perseverance to keep at it so long, to work so hard without giving up?

We're going to delve in a little to find out how Musk does this while staying organized at the same time.

First of all, Musk believes in batching, combining several tasks and doing them simultaneously. This allows an individual to get more tasks accomplished in his day.

Musk also cuts time from his lunch break, keeping his time away from the job under half an hour. While he's having lunch, he is e-mailing or having meetings at the same time, to bring his productivity to a higher level. He sometimes combines writing e-mails with looking over spreadsheets, especially if he needs to look at spreadsheets for some of the e-mails anyway.

Musk pointed out:

> *"But what I find is I'm able to be with (my kids) and still be on email. I can be with them and still be working at the same time ... If I didn't, I wouldn't be able to get my job done."*

Secondly, Musk doesn't waste energy on advertisements. If you've never seen many billboards or television shows advertising Tesla, that's probably because there aren't many. Why not? Musk is more concerned about spending energy and money on making better products than spending them on advertisements. He figures that if the product is great, people will want it, even without the high costs of advertising.

> *"A lot of companies get confused; they spend money on things that don't actually make the product better."*

In the end, Musk realized that no matter how great the advertising, if the product is less than ideal, a company will have trouble selling it long-term. On the same note, there is no need to advertise a truly great product. News will spread on its own when people love it and are sold on it.

Thirdly, Musk has discovered that it is important to base the work day around a tightly organized schedule. When you stick to the schedule closely, this allows people to be more productive, and is a main secret of Musk's companies' successes.

Because he oversees two companies, a closely held schedule is that much more important. Musk's daily planner is broken into five minute slots, allowing him to micromanage his day's work. His personal aide saves him hours of work by bringing his tasks to him.

With Musk's crazy schedule, he spends Mondays and Thursdays in Los Angeles working with SpaceX, and Tuesday through Wednesday in the

Bay Area, working at Tesla. Fridays he splits between the two companies, with SpaceX and then at the headquarters of Tesla, which is adjacent. This schedule cuts down on his commuting time, making him more efficient in his work.

Finally, Musk admitted sometimes he uses stimulants to help him function. He used to drink up to eight cans of Diet coke daily, and several cups of coffee on top of that. Now Musk finds that the driving dreams he has to change the world help stimulate him enough that he can cut back on the others.

Lesson # 8 – On having Fun

"Everybody around here has slides in their lobbies. I'm actually wondering about putting in a roller coaster — like a functional roller coaster at the factory in Fremont. You'd get in, and it would take you around [the] factory but also up and down. Who else has a roller coaster? ... It would probably be really expensive, but I like the idea of it."

Quote context:

Interview with Ashlee Vance for the book: "Elon Musk: Tesla, SpaceX, and the Quest for a Fantastic

Future", published May 19, 2015

Meaning of the quote:

Some people are a bit too uptight. They take their businesses and their personal lives too seriously. Wanting to achieve more, they tend to think that every drop of pleasure or enjoyment would somehow cost them.

The fact is business and fun do not necessarily have to be separated. Studies have shown that employees who have fun in the workplace, from belly laughs and birthday celebrations to video games and massages, take less sick leave, work harder and are more productive.

Lessons from Elon Musk:

No one can deny that Musk's schedule is insane. Sometimes working as much as 100 hours in one week, Musk rarely has time to take a break or go on vacation. He is kept constantly busy, trying to juggle the various tasks laid upon him by being head of multiple companies simultaneously.

Is Musk a serious and severe man with no time for fun? Definitely not! His sense of humor bubbles through, even despite the long hours and heavy responsibilities.

Musk plans to build a giant rollercoaster for the offices of SpaceX and Tesla. Musk had seen how some technology companies such as YouTube or Google had incorporated elements into their work environments, such as plants, treadmills, pianos, and slides, to make the workplace a more relaxing and enjoyable place for everyone. Musk had his own idea: a roller coaster.

While this may catch a few off guard, Musk is really a good sport who enjoys having fun. As a kid, he spent a lot of time playing video games or reading comic books, which he still enjoys in his free time. Recently, he mentioned a number of games he enjoys as well:

> *"FPS with a story, like Bioshock, Fallout or Mass Effect, but was also a big fan of Civ (Civilization, a Real-time Strategy Game) and Warcraft."*

When he has time on the weekends, he enjoys having fun with his five children. Some activities they enjoy doing together are building a model rocket or going to see a movie. One of the more unusual activities that Musk and his children worked on together was his own form of the ALS

Ice Bucket Challenge. This campaign, which went viral in 2015, created awareness for those with amyotrophic lateral sclerosis. Musk's participation included building a contraption that would dump five buckets of ice water, representing each of his five children, on his head simultaneously. He then put a video of this event on SpaceX's YouTube channel.

Musk also takes some time for TV, as well as movies, although books are still his favorite. He has even agreed to appear on several shows. For example, in 2005, he appeared in the "Thank You for Smoking" film, with a cameo of piloting his own plane. In his role, he opened the door for Robert Duvall, playing The Captain, and escorted Aaron Eckhart (who was playing Nick Naylor) on board the plane.

He appeared again in 2010 on the Iron Man 2 show. In this appearance, Musk went to a restaurant, where he met Robert Downey Jr. (as Tony Stark), and made a few statements about his "idea for an electric jet". The film's producer, Jon Favreau, admitted that he had partially modeled the main character based on the inspiration from Elon Musk's life. Musk also allowed several scenes in the movie to be filmed of SpaceX's facilities.

Musk's acting career did not end with these two movies. In 2013, Musk appeared briefly in "Machete Kills", pretending to be himself. Musk greets the main character of the movie as he is about to board a Falcon 9 that SpaceX had built. The main character is chasing the antagonist of the film, and Musk encourages him as he shakes Machete's hand: "Good luck Machete, kill the bastard."

In 2014, his role in the film Transcendence was simple—sitting there and listening to Paul Bettany.

Although the main purpose of "The Musk Who Fell to Earth" was to make fun of several of his ideas, Musk agreed to play himself in this episode of The Simpsons in January 2015.

Once again in November of 2015, Musk played himself in one episode of the show The Big Bang Theory, where he volunteered in a soup kitchen with one of the characters in the show, Howard. Later he claimed that he enjoyed the series.

Lesson # 9 – On Changing the World

"When I was in college, I wanted to be involved in things that would change the world. Now I am."

Quote context:

Interview at the D11 Conference, May 2013

Meaning of the quote:

Don't underestimate the power of dreams. Look at the world around you. All that we have achieved today is the result of small things that started out as nothing but mere dreams, or in other words, vision: A vision to make the world a better place.

Dream big. Have a vision of what you want to change, and start taking action. Couple that vision with unrelenting determination and hard work, and watch as world changing events happen through your hands.

Lessons from Elon Musk:

Elon Musk is characterized by dreaming big. His dreams involve three main areas: sustainable energy, the Internet, and exploring space with the end of allowing multi-planetary travel.

So far, we've explored how Musk is working to reinvent the automobile, how he worked to develop the internet, how he's making progress in exploring space, and how he's trying new ideas to develop high speed railways. But there's one thing we've failed to mention yet in our list of ways he's changing the world in drastic ways: work in the field of sustainable energy.

Musk's work to develop the electric car wasn't an end in itself, but merely a step in his overarching hope to allow the whole world to find a way to provide and store clean energy on a mass scale.

The internet took a huge turn in the 1990s, and now Musk hopes to do the same in the energy specter. The whole world has received access to information, and Musk wants to provide clean energy to just as many people.

Tesla Energy, a new branch of Tesla, opened in 2015. Musk announced the first product this new branch would deliver: the Powerwall. Small enough it can hang on the wall, this Powerwall stores energy it absorbs from the power grid or from the sun during daylight hours. This energy is then released at evening or at peak times of energy use.

The Powerwall isn't the only sustainable energy product that Musk has developed. Even SolarCity was developed based on ideas that Musk gave to Lyndon and Peter Rive, his cousins. Once they established the company, he helped chair and lead it as it grew exponentially to be one of the US's major solar companies. Lyndon Rive, one of the founders points out that they are developing an industry where people can work at "greencollar" jobs.

In August of 2016, a deal Musk had proposed two months earlier finally solidified, allowing him to purchase SolarCity to integrate it with Tesla Motors. This would allow the creation of "a seamlessly integrated Tesla battery & solar power product that looks beautiful". Musk hopes that by combining the two companies into the world's first vertically sustainable energy company, he can accomplish even greater things going forward.

They hope to create a "solar roof" to harvest the sun's energy. Musk states:

"We have this handy fusion reactor in the sky called the Sun. You don't have to do anything, it just works."

Lesson # 10 – On the Future

"If you go back a few hundred years, what we take for granted today would seem like magic – being able to talk to people over long distances, to transmit images, flying, accessing vast amounts of data like an oracle. These are all things that would have been considered magic a few hundred years ago."

Quote context:

Interview with Forbes reporter Hannah Elliot, March 26, 2013

Meaning of the quote:

Science fiction writer, Arthur C. Clarke once declared: "Any sufficiently advanced technology is indistinguishable from magic."

This is true in so many ways. Today we take the technology around us for granted, without really realizing that a lot of what we have around now seemed impossible a few centuries ago. Things that were written in classical science fiction are now part of our daily lives.

And we still have not stopped there. Breakthroughs are being made on a daily basis. The possibilities are endless. To believe a thing impossible is to make it so. Change is possible only when you envision the world as a world of possibilities and discover a way around the problems to achieve those possibilities.

Lessons from Elon Musk:

Have you ever thought back to when you were a child, listening to the classic stories at bedtime, stories that describe genies who could click their fingers and send you to a distant place? Or maybe you fondly remember the Sci-Fi TV shows where the characters could teleport themselves to another galaxy at the speed of light. While science has not attained to these feats described in science fiction and fairy tales, real life has made considerable progress in that direction.

Elon Musk has done what seemed impossible in the field of electric cars, developing advanced space rocket technology, and allowing people to transfer money instantly. What other surprises might Musk still have for us? His latest experiment, the Hyperloop project, is one of those things. Generally speaking, Hyperloop is a fifth means of man-made self-propelled transportation, coming onto the scene of history after trains, planes, cars, and boats. While you could technically include rockets as a means of transportation, most people never get the chance to travel on one, so we won't count them for this purpose.

In the Hyperloop transportation system, passengers get into a pressurized capsule, and sit inside while the capsule is transported by a cushion of air, by vacuum force. Musk has not yet finalized how to propel this capsule; two options he has considered are air pressure or magnetized levitation. Musk describes his invention as a type of train of the future, "a cross between a Concorde, a rail gun and an air hockey table". Musk believes that his new form of transportation will allow people to travel at 560 miles an hour (900 kilometers per hour), or even as fast as 760 miles an hour (1220 kilometers per hour).

This project is more than Musk can currently take on, with all the other projects he's working on, so he has decided to give away this idea, allowing competition to build. Student-led all-star disciplinary teams have begun to work together to develop this technology, as well as several companies.

What is Musk's point in doing all of this? He explains:

> *"What we really intended to do with the Hyperloop was really to just spur interest in new forms of transportation and I think this is really gonna happen. It's clear that the public, the world, wants something new..."*

How did Musk come up with such a novel idea? In an interview, he stated that he first dreamed up this concept while stuck in a traffic jam in Los Angeles. The traffic was backed up so far that he arrived at his meeting a whole hour late. This delay was enough to stir up his problem solving determination. Musk declared his decision to invent a fifth method of transportation at a Santa Monica, California PandoDaily event. But why is this method of transportation more advantageous than any of the others?

Hyperloop offers several advantages:

- One major advantage is that the pressurized capsules theoretically cannot crash.
- Hyperloop transportation would also save money, costing only a tenth of the price of the high-speed railway that California proposed. This could potentially bring ticket prices down to 25 dollars.
- Hyperloop is also much faster than trains, allowing travel from Los Angeles to San Francisco in as little as half an hour.

- Using solar energy allows the Hyperloop system to be extremely efficient, perhaps generating more power than it uses up to transport people, thus generating power.

Of course, any new system has problems to work through, and critics have already identified a few potential challenges:

- Passengers might be fearful of riding through a steel tunnel, narrowly confined in a windowless sealed capsule.
- Passengers might experience motion sickness because of noisy vibration or quick acceleration.
- There could be potential problems dealing with accidents, emergency evacuations, or equipment malfunctioning.
- Costs to build the Hyperloop system might not be as low as originally believed.

These problems raised by the critics were not ideas unfamiliar to Musk. As usual, he had thought of potential problems, but was confident that they could be addressed through the innovation and skills of those who were working out the kinks in the system and improving the design.

This idea, surprisingly enough, was not original to Musk. George Medhurst, a British inventor and engineer, described such a system in 1812. In 1864, London opened three tunnels that ran on steam engine power, using large fans. This system successfully operated for around a year before it closed.

At the time this book was written, Hyperloop tracks are under construction in Nevada, where engineers are using them to test and refine their systems and designs. SpaceX, as well as two other companies, have initiated funding rounds to allow the Hyperloop to operate. These companies also are communicating with governments in different major cities around the world, encouraging them to build Hyperloops for their populations.

Young designers, inventors, and engineers have a bright future with the opportunities that Elon Musk has brought into existence. If they can get plugged into building the Hyperloop system, they could change the history of transportation.

It's also refreshing to see Musk sharing his ideas openly, allowing others to innovate within this infrastructure. While most try to patent their ideas, Musk is doing something radically different, allowing others to take and develop and bring into reality what seems like a magical idea, the Hyperloop.

Conclusion

Congratulations and thank you again for purchasing this book and reading it all the way to this point!

Elon Musk is not your ordinary billionaire. Unlike most, Musk has made billions of dollars multiple times with entirely different businesses. I hope you have learned something valuable from his inspiring life story.

Finally, if you enjoyed this book, then I'd like to ask you for a favor, would you be kind enough to leave a review for this book on Amazon? Tell us what you like or dislike and what we can improve. Your feedbacks will be greatly appreciated!

https://www.amazon.com

Also follow EntrepreneurshipFacts on social media to stay updated with our new books and increase your knowledge about business and successful people on a daily basis:

Instagram   Facebook   Twitter

Check out our website for the latest facts and articles about business and entrepreneurship:

www.EntrepreneurshipFacts.com

More books by Entrepreneurship Facts

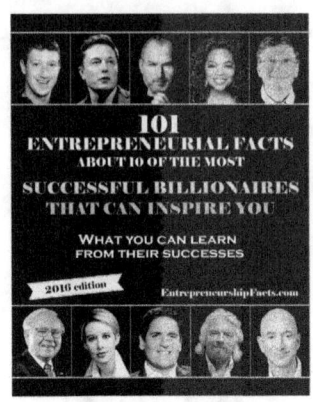

101 Entrepreneurial Facts About 10 of The Most Successful BILLIONAIRES That Can Inspire You: What you can learn from their successes

The Real Life RICH DAD & The Lessons He Taught ROBERT KIYOSAKI about Money

Warren Buffett - 41 Fascinating Facts about Life & Investing Philosophy: The Lessons From A Legendary Investor

www.ingramcontent.com/pod-product-compliance
Lightning Source LLC
Chambersburg PA
CBHW060402190526
45169CB00002B/711